# Time to Go

I Talk You Talk Press

# CONTENTS

I Talk You Talk Press

# CHAPTER ONE

Dan looked out of the big glass window of his office in downtown Kowloon, Hong Kong. He could see Hong Kong Island. The lights from the buildings on the island glowed brightly against the November sky. The heavy rain was hitting the windows, and the sky was growing darker.

*A perfect night,* he thought.

He walked over to his office door and looked through the narrow window into the main office. He could see Nancy Peng, his accountant, and the other four employees. They were working at their desks, looking at their computer screens and talking on telephones.

"I'm sorry," he said very quietly. He went back to his desk and sat down.

A message flashed on Dan's screen. It was from Nancy.

---*Dan, we need to talk about the company accounts before the end of the month. What time is best for you tomorrow?*---

Dan deleted the message and switched the computer off.

"I'm sorry Nancy," he said to himself quietly. "I have to do this."

He closed his eyes. A phone was ringing in the main office. The two workers at the desks nearest to his door were talking in loud voices about some numbers. The rain was getting stronger.

Dan opened his eyes, stood up and put on his black jacket. Then, he opened his office door and walked into the main office.

"Dan," said Nancy. "Did you get my message?"

Dan did not answer her. He walked out of the door and got into an elevator.

1

On the ground floor, the elevator doors opened. Dan walked out of the elevator.

"Good evening Mr Hamilton," said the building receptionist.

Dan did not answer. He walked across the lobby, and out through the doors into the wet evening. He hurried through the crowds. Most people had umbrellas. He looked up at the sky. The neon lights glowed red, blue and yellow. The windows in the office buildings were very bright.

*Hong Kong,* thought Dan. *I'm going to miss this city.*

He walked into a car park.

"Good evening, Mr Hamilton" said the car park attendant.

Dan did not answer.

He got into his black sports car and drove out of the car park. It was 6:00pm. The roads were very busy. There were many cars and trucks on the roads.

He drove onto a main highway and followed the signs for the Container Port. Soon, he could see the lights of the port and the ships, cranes and containers.

*Nearly there,* he thought. He could see the bridge in front of him.

*This is it,* he thought.

There were many cars and trucks on the bridge. The wind was strong, and the rain was so heavy, that it was difficult to see. He drove slowly in the left lane on the bridge.

*Here,* he thought. He suddenly stopped the car at the side of the road.

People in the other cars and trucks sounded their horns. Some of them tried to look at him. The rain poured down on the car and the window. Soon, he couldn't see anything. He put his wallet and his mobile phone on the passenger seat.

He opened the door on the passenger side. The wind hit his face very hard. He couldn't breathe very well. He got out of the car and shut the car door. It was very noisy on the bridge. The cars, the trucks, the wind and the rain were noisy. The lights on the bridge were very bright. He walked along the side of the bridge. Then, he stopped and looked down over the railings. He could see very large ships in the port. He could hear and see the dark water below the bridge. He leant over the cold railings. A car driver sounded his horn.

Another driver shouted, "Hey! What are you doing?"

Someone else shouted, "Stop!"

There were many cars on the bridge, so no-one could stop. But they saw him.

Dan looked down at the water.

*It's time,* he thought. *It's time to go...*

The police arrived at the bridge. They called for the rescue team. They closed the bridge and a helicopter came. They searched the dark water for Dan for many hours that night. But they didn't find Dan. He was gone.

# CHAPTER TWO

Nancy Peng sat in Dan's chair in his office. She turned around and looked out of the window. It was a sunny day. The rain from the night before had gone. Nancy looked up at the blue sky. Then she closed her eyes. She was very tired. She hadn't slept very well. She and the other workers had been working late in the office when the police came.

"Daniel Hamilton is dead", they said. "He jumped off a bridge. We found his car, but we didn't find his body."

Nancy couldn't believe it. She had told the other employees to go home and take a holiday the next day. That night, she had stayed in the office. She had been too shocked to go home. She had tried to sleep in the soft chairs in the meeting room, but she couldn't sleep.

She had woken up early and made some coffee. She had many things to do.

Nancy thought about her boss, Dan.

*I don't know much about him,* she thought. *He was a really private person. We sometimes went out for lunch or dinner together and we had a nice time. But we usually talked about business. He didn't talk about his private life at all.*

Dan was an Australian man who had come to Hong Kong and set up his company. Nancy had worked for him for a long time. They were almost like business partners. Nancy knew that he was single and lived in the expensive area, the Peak, on Hong Kong Island. He had a nice apartment, a sports car, and a successful business. The business didn't have any problems.

*So why did he kill himself?* Nancy didn't understand. *And why didn't he talk to me? Maybe I could have helped him.*

The police said it was not unusual. People disappear all the time. People kill themselves. Often, they have money problems. Many people saw Dan getting out of his sports car on the bridge. Some people saw him leaning over the railings.

"But did you find his body?" Nancy had asked the police.

"No, we haven't found a body. It is difficult to find bodies in that water," they had said.

Nancy looked at the clock on the office wall. It was 9:30am.

*I have to go to the bank,* she thought. *I have to tell the bank manager about Dan. And I have to check the money in the company bank account.*

She put her jacket on and walked out of the office. She locked the door behind her. She got in the elevator and went down to the lobby. She said hello to the receptionist. She left the building and walked out onto the busy street. There was a man standing at the entrance to the building. He was wearing a dark blue suit. He didn't look at her.

The bank was not far from the office. Nancy walked in and stood in the line. It was not so busy, and she was soon at the front of the line.

"Good morning Ms Peng," said the cashier.

"Good morning. I need to talk to the manager," said Nancy. "But first, could you tell me the balance of this account?" She gave the cashier the bank account number.

"Just a moment," said the cashier. She printed out a piece of paper. "Here you are."

Nancy looked at the paper.

"What?" she said.

"Is something wrong, Ms Peng?" asked the cashier.

The paper showed that $250,000 had been taken out of the US dollar account. She looked at the date. It was yesterday. The day Dan disappeared.

"Excuse me," she said to the cashier. "But...who took this money? Who took two hundred and fifty thousand dollars from the company bank account?"

The cashier looked at her computer. "Mr Daniel Hamilton took it out," she said. "He wanted it all in cash."

"But why?"

The cashier looked at her. "I don't know," she said. "He didn't say. Is there a problem?"

"Well… actually…oh it doesn't matter," said Nancy.

*The cashier hasn't heard about Dan jumping from the bridge,* thought Nancy. She didn't want to tell her.

"Are you sure it was Mr Hamilton?" she said.

"Yes," said the cashier. "Only Mr Hamilton and you can take money out of the account."

"Are you really sure it was him?" Nancy asked again.

The cashier looked at her. "Yes, I am. I was here yesterday. I served him!"

"Do you have a record of this?" asked Nancy.

"Of course."

The cashier went to a cabinet. She came back with a piece of paper. It had a signature on it.

Nancy looked at it closely. She recognised the signature. It was definitely Dan's signature.

*But why did he take out two hundred and fifty thousand dollars on the day he killed himself? Was he in trouble? Did he have to pay someone?*

"So, Ms Peng, you would like to see the manager?" asked the cashier. "He is in a meeting now, but he can see you at ten thirty."

"No, it's OK," said Nancy. "I'll come back another day. Thanks."

She thought it was strange. She wanted some time to think. She put the paper in her bag.

"Thank you, Ms Peng," said the cashier.

Nancy walked towards the door. There were some people waiting to use the cash machine. Nancy noticed one of them.

*Who is he? I've seen him before,* she thought. That's it! *That man was standing outside my office building. It's the same man. Did he follow me?*

Nancy walked out of the bank and stood next to the door. She took her smartphone out of her bag and looked at it. She watched the man. He took some money out of the cash machine and walked out of the bank. He didn't look at her. He walked down the road and disappeared into the crowd.

*Maybe he is just a businessman. Maybe he didn't follow me,* she thought.

She walked back to the office. The sun felt warm on her face, but there was a strong wind.

Nancy went into the office and locked the door. She walked into Dan's office and switched on his computer. She looked at his emails, but there was nothing unusual. All the emails were communication with clients.

She looked through all the drawers in his desk, but she didn't find anything strange. Dan had gone. And he had taken $250,000 with him.

# CHAPTER THREE

Jason sat in the lounge area on the deck of his yacht. A cup of coffee was on the table next to the chair. He put down his smartphone and looked at Hong Kong Island. The morning mist was clearing from the top of Victoria Peak.

*The Peak...* he thought. Jason had many good memories of the Peak. His first friend in Hong Kong, Dan, lived there. They sometimes had house parties. But that was a long time ago. Dan's business became successful, and Dan started to work more and more. He had no time for Jason. They hadn't seen each other for years.

*And now he's dead,* thought Jason. He had received an email from another friend. Dan had jumped from a bridge last night.

*Why?* he thought. *Was he in trouble?*

Jason drank his coffee. He knew about trouble. Before he bought his yacht, he borrowed some money from an Australian man called Harry. Harry was the leader of a group. The group lent people money. They were not nice people. They told Jason he had to pay back a lot more money than he had borrowed. Jason had a lot of trouble after that. He still hadn't paid them all the money they wanted. He was paying a little every month.

His smartphone rang. He looked at it. He didn't know the number on the screen.

"Hello?" he said.

"Jason, it's me," said the voice.

"Who?" asked Jason.

"It's me. Dan Hamilton," said the voice.

"What? But…but…you are dead!" said Jason.

"Listen Jason, I can't talk now. I'm not dead. I'm alive. I need your help," said Dan.

"But…where are you? And why…the bridge…what? I don't understand," said Jason.

"Jason. I need your yacht. I need you to take me to Australia. I need you to take me out of Hong Kong. I need you to do it today. Now. I'll explain later. It's very important. Can you do it?"

"I don't know," said Jason. "Is it really you Dan? This isn't a joke?"

"Jason it's me! Please Jason! I need your help. Can you do it?"

Jason thought about it for a few seconds.

*I can get some money,* he thought.

"Well, yes, I think so, but… it isn't cheap," said Jason. "It will be expensive to take the yacht all the way to Australia and I might be in danger – the police are looking for you in the water. And if you want to leave Hong Kong, I guess other people, some bad people, are looking for you too."

"I'll pay you. I'll give you fifty thousand US dollars," said Dan.

Jason thought about it.

"Only fifty thousand? It will cost you more than that."

"Seventy-five thousand US dollars?"

"Hmm…I don't know…."

"OK, OK. A hundred thousand?"

"OK. I can do it," said Jason. "But you must tell me why."

"Jason, I'm in trouble. It's a long story."

"Tell me," said Jason.

"OK. I have bought many apartments in Hong Kong. I rent them to foreign businessmen. I made a lot of money. A month ago, I bought a new apartment for myself. It was expensive and I used most of my money. Then about a week ago, a man came to see me. He said his name was Paul. He said 'I can get you a luxury apartment for a good price. You can buy the apartment for half the real price.' I thought it was very strange. I said 'I don't have enough money, but I will think about it. Maybe I can borrow the extra money because it is a very good price.' He said, 'My friend can lend you the money.' I said, 'I will call you in a few days.'

"I found out who owned the apartment. He bought it about six weeks ago for a quarter of its real price. Then I found he had bought other apartments at very, very low prices. I found the original owners of the apartments and talked to them. They were all older people. They said 'Scary men came to see us. The men said, If you do not sell your apartments for a very low price, we will find your families in Hong Kong and China and kill them.' The old people were too frightened to go to the police.

"I was so angry. Those old people lost their homes. I thought, *I can help them. I can meet the men and tell them to give the old people money.* So I did a very stupid thing. I didn't go to the police. I called Paul. I said, 'I want to buy the apartment. I want to borrow money from your friend.' I met Paul and his friend in a restaurant. The friend was his boss. He is not a nice man. I said, 'I know everything. I will tell the police.' The boss became very angry. He said, 'You are a dead man!' He said, 'You cannot hide from me in Hong Kong. I have friends in the police. If you talk to the police, I will know about it.'

"I ran out of the restaurant. They followed me, but I was lucky and got away. I thought, *If they think I am dead, I will be safe.* I had an idea. I jumped from the bridge. It was not too high. I was wearing a lifejacket. But I must get away from Hong Kong. You have to help me."

Jason listened carefully. "Dan, what was the name of the man who came to see you?"

"Paul. But the boss is Harry. He's an Australian. And he's very dangerous."

Jason thought for a moment. "Dan, I need to think about this. Can I call you back?"

"Yes. You can use this number. It's a pre-paid mobile phone."

"I'll call you back later," said Jason. He hung up and walked into the living area of the yacht. He poured himself a whisky and sat on the sofa. He thought very carefully about everything. Fifteen minutes later, he called Dan.

"Dan, listen. I can do it," said Jason. "But I have some things to do today. Meet me at my yacht in the harbour at twelve midnight. My yacht is the green one at the far end of the harbour. Don't forget the money."

"Sure. Thanks Jason."

Jason hung up. Then, he called Harry.

# CHAPTER FOUR

Nancy woke up.

The intercom was ringing. She looked around. She was still sitting in Dan's office. She looked at the clock. 11:00am.

*I fell asleep,* she thought.

She walked into the main office and picked up the phone. It was the receptionist in the lobby on the ground floor.

"Ms Peng, there are two people here to see you. They are from the Australian Embassy."

"Send them up," said Nancy. She rubbed her eyes and put her suit jacket on. She walked to the door and waited for them.

They came out of the elevator. There was an Australian man and a Chinese man. They walked into the office.

"Good afternoon," said the Australian man. "I'm Tim Blake. I'm from the Australian Embassy. This is my co-worker, Paul Fu."

"Good afternoon," said Nancy. "Come in."

She took them into the meeting room.

"Would you like some tea?" she asked.

"No, it's OK. We won't stay long," said Tim.

They sat down.

"It must be a terrible shock for you," said Tim. "I'm so sorry to hear about your boss. But, we need your help. We contacted Dan's family in Australia. They are very upset, and are looking for answers."

"I'm sure they are," said Nancy. "But I don't have any answers. I don't know why Dan would kill himself."

"We would like you to talk to us," said Paul.

11

Nancy looked at him. "I don't know anything. Dan was a very private person. I didn't know him very well. But the business is fine. I don't understand it."

"Was he in trouble?" asked Tim.

"I don't think so," said Nancy.

"Did he have any strange business deals?"

"No, I don't think so. He was buying an apartment on Hong Kong Island. But he bought many apartments. That wasn't strange."

"Do you have the address for the new apartment?" asked Paul.

"No, I don't. The apartments are private investments. They have no connection to the company."

"Did any strange people come to visit him?" asked Tim.

"No. No one. I don't know about his private life, but he didn't seem to have any trouble here. And he spent all his time here in this office. I don't think he had any free time."

"Was he depressed?"

"He didn't seem depressed," said Nancy. "He seemed fine. I'm sorry. I really don't know anything."

"I know this is very hard for you," said Tim. "But his family is so upset. His mother can't believe her son has died."

"He never spoke about his mother," said Nancy. "But I'm sure she must be very upset."

"Oh she is very upset. And she is very sick. Dan's brother said, 'She will not live much longer. She will die soon. She really needs to know.' Anything you can tell us. Anything at all."

Nancy thought about it. She imagined Dan's mother. She was sick, and very upset about her son.

"Well," she said. "There is something strange. I just went to the bank. Yesterday, before he died, Dan took two hundred and fifty thousand dollars in cash out of the company US dollar account."

Tim and Paul looked at each other.

"Oh really?" said Paul. "What did he do with it?"

"I don't know," said Nancy. "Because then he jumped off the bridge."

The two men looked at each other again.

"Maybe he was in trouble. Did you tell the police?" asked Tim.

"No, I didn't," said Nancy. "What can the police do? Dan took money from his own company bank account. That is not a crime."

"Well, you should not go to the police," said Tim. "We will talk to

12

the police. At the embassy, we have a lot of experience. People get into trouble all the time. People often disappear. We have experts at the embassy. If the police need information, we will come with you and help you when you talk to them."

"OK, thanks," said Nancy.

"I know this is hard for you," said Tim. "Thank you for meeting with us today. We'll contact you again. And if you think of anything else, please let us know. Dan's mother is so upset. Here is my direct number. Don't call the embassy number. Call me directly on this number."

Tim gave Nancy a piece of paper with a mobile phone number on it.

"Yes, of course," said Nancy. "Thank you." She put it in her pocket.

The men walked out of the office and into the elevator.

Nancy walked to the window. She looked down on the street below. She saw the men walk out of the office building. A big black car was waiting for them.

The driver got out of the car and opened the back door.

"Oh!" said Nancy. *He looks like that man...in the bank...*she thought. *Is it the same man?*

Tim and Paul got into the car. Nancy watched as the car drove away down the busy road.

# CHAPTER FIVE

Dan walked around his new apartment. He could not relax.

*I have to wait until midnight,* he thought. *But that's fine. That's OK. No one knows I am here. No one knows about this apartment. I only bought it a month ago.* He walked to the window. The apartment had great views of the city. The sky was blue and there were no clouds. It was a beautiful day.

Dan thought about the night before. During the day, he had taken the money out of the bank and taken it to his new apartment. Then, he had taken a motorbike to the port and parked it in the parking area near the bridge. He had driven to the bridge in his sports car. The bridge was not so high. He had leaned over the railings. Many people had seen him. Then, he had jumped. He had been wearing a lifejacket under his coat, so he could float. Then, he had swum to a dark part of the port and jumped on the motorbike and ridden to this luxury apartment. He had bought the apartment only a month before. It was near the one Harry wanted to sell him.

He sat down on the soft carpet in the living room and closed his eyes.

*Tonight, at midnight, I will escape,* he thought. *Harry and his group will never find me. I can go back to Australia and start again. Get a new name. Start a new business. I will be fine.*

Then he thought about Nancy and the other workers. *I feel really bad. I walked out on them. They think I am dead. But I will write to Nancy when I get back to Australia. I hope she will understand. The company account has two hundred thousand US dollars in it. I'll write her a letter. I'll tell her to*

14

*close the business and keep the money. But I'll miss her. She is a good worker, and I think we were slowly becoming friends.*

Dan was a shy man. He didn't make friends very easily. When he first came to Hong Kong, he tried to make friends. He went to parties. That was when he met Jason. But he was naturally shy. He found it difficult to talk to women. But he liked talking to Nancy. He felt he could trust her. He looked out of the window to the other side of the city.

"I'm sorry Nancy," he said quietly. "I hope you are not sad. I hope you and the other workers will be OK."

On the other side of the city, Nancy was searching Dan's office. There was a locked cabinet. She wanted to find the key. At last she found it in Dan's desk drawer under a notepad. She looked at the clock. It was lunchtime. She was hungry and very tired. There was a coffee shop across the street.

*I'll have a coffee and sandwich,* she thought. *Then I'll search Dan's office.*

Nancy walked across the road and into the coffee shop. There were many people. She joined the line and waited.

At last, she was at the front of the line.

"Yes, what would you like?" asked the man behind the counter.

"A double espresso and a cheese and tomato sandwich please," said Nancy. She took out her purse to pay. When she took her purse out of her pocket, she didn't notice Tim's business card fall on the floor. She paid and carried her coffee and sandwich on a tray to a table next to the window. She drank the espresso and ate the sandwich. Then, she walked out of the coffee shop and went back to the office. She took the elevator up to the office and locked the door. She unlocked the filing cabinet and looked through the papers.

She found the papers for Dan's apartments. She found the rental contracts. She found a folder about Dan's new apartment. She wrote down the address. But there was another folder with just one piece of paper in it.

*What's this?* she thought. There was a list of addresses. The one at the top had a lot of question marks next to it. And Dan had written,

*---Half price!---*

*I should tell Tim about this,* she thought. She put her hand in her pocket. *Where is Tim's phone number? Maybe I dropped it in the coffee shop. It's OK. I can just call the Australian Embassy.* She sat in front of the computer and found the Australian Embassy website on the Internet. She picked up the phone and called the number on the website.

"Hello, I'd like to speak to Tim Blake, please," said Nancy.

"Tim Blake? No one called Tim Blake works here," said the embassy employee.

"Oh, really? Well, OK, could I speak to Mr Paul Fu instead, please?" asked Nancy.

"There is no one called Paul Fu here," said the employee.

"OK, thanks," said Nancy. She put the phone down.

*Something is wrong. Something is very wrong,* she thought. *Who is Tim Blake? And who is Paul Fu? They are not embassy workers. Why were they looking for information? And, what about the money that Dan took? And the man in the bank? Who was he?* Nancy started to feel frightened.

*Dan is alive,* she thought. *Dan is alive. And he is in trouble. I can feel it. But where is he?*

She walked over to the window and looked out at the busy city. *And how can I find him in this city of millions of people? Where would you go if everyone thought you were dead? You could go anywhere. Has he left Hong Kong? Probably. Are his friends helping him?*

She sat down again.

*Does he have friends? He worked 16 hours a day. He had no time for friends. And he never spoke about friends. I have to find Dan,* she thought. *He is in danger. Maybe he is hiding in one of his apartments. Most of them are rented to people. Maybe he is hiding in his new apartment. Or maybe he bought this one that says 'half-price!' and he is hiding there. I could go and see.*

Nancy took the file and ran into the reception area. One of her co-workers, Sarah, had left her jacket and hat in the office. The coat was red. She put Sarah's coat on and tied her long hair up. She put Sarah's hat on. Then, she walked out of the office. She locked the office door and got in the elevator.

The elevator stopped at the fifth floor. Some other office workers got in the elevator. At the ground floor, Nancy walked out with them. The man across the road watching the building didn't recognise Nancy. When she got to the end of the road, she turned around. The man was still waiting outside the office building.

*He didn't recognise me,* she thought. She ran down the metro station steps and into the underground metro station.

# CHAPTER SIX

Nancy ran up the metro station steps into the late afternoon sun. She was on Hong Kong Island. The 'half-price' apartment was just a short walk from the station. She pulled the collar of Sarah's jacket around her face, and walked quickly to the apartment block.

She looked up at the apartment block. It had 40 floors. The apartment was on the 39th floor. She went into the lobby.

"Good afternoon, madam," said the building manager.

Nancy smiled at him and walked to the elevator. She got in the elevator and pressed 38.

The elevator rose to the 38th floor. She got out of the elevator. She was in a long hall. There were two doors on the right side. On the left side, there were large windows with views of the city. At the far end of the hall, there were some stairs. She walked to the stairs and very quietly, walked up to the 39th floor.

There were two apartments. 39A and 39B. The 'half-price' apartment was 39B. Very quietly, she walked along the hall until she reached 39B.

The door was closed, but she could smell cigarette smoke coming from the apartment.

*Someone is in there. But who is it?* she thought. *Dan doesn't smoke.*

She put her ear next to the door. She could hear voices. They were speaking in English.

She tried to listen carefully.

"The manager said a woman went to the thirty-eighth floor. She was wearing a red jacket. So it's not her. She has a black jacket."

17

"I saw a red jacket in the reception area when I went to the office," said another man.

*I know that voice. It's Paul Fu!* thought Nancy.

"So? Many people wear red jackets," said the other man. "And Wei is waiting outside her office. He will call if she goes out. It's not her."

"We should go Dan's new apartment, Harry," said Paul. "We can kill him there."

Harry? Who's Harry? thought Nancy.

"Relax! Jason's yacht is the best place. It's better to kill Dan on a boat. We can punch and kick him until he dies. Then, we can throw his body into the water. Everyone thinks he jumped off the bridge, so it won't seem strange. Let's just wait. He will be at Jason's boat before midnight. We will leave the harbour at midnight, and then a few hours later, we kill him. Easy."

Nancy was shocked. *Kill Dan?* she thought. *I must find him!*

Then, the elevator door opened. She turned around. It was the building manager.

"What are you doing?" he asked. "Hey!"

Nancy ran towards the man. She pushed him and he fell into the wall. Then, she got in the elevator and pressed the ground floor button.

"Hey! Stop!" shouted the manager. He tried to stop the elevator, but the doors closed.

"Come on! Faster!" Nancy said to the elevator. "Faster!"

The elevator stopped at the thirteenth floor.

"Oh no!" she said. "Come on!"

A man and a woman got in the elevator. She didn't look at them. The doors closed. Then the elevator started to go down. On the ground floor, the elevator doors opened. Nancy said, "Excuse me," and ran out of the elevator, pushing the man and woman out of the way. She ran out of the apartment building and looked up. There were two men on the balcony of the apartment on the 39th floor. They were watching her. She ran towards the metro station.

# CHAPTER SEVEN

Wei was bored. It was 4:00pm. He had been standing outside the office building all day.

*What time will she go home?* he thought. *I hope she comes out soon. I'm cold.*

Then, his phone rang. He looked at the number. It was Harry.

"Hello Harry. Wei speaking," said Wei.

"What are you doing? She is here! Didn't you see her?" shouted Harry.

Wei was very shocked. "What? But, Harry, she hasn't come out of the office building. She is still there!"

"No, she isn't! She was here, just a few minutes ago! The manager of this building said she was listening to us! She knows about the plan! We must catch her!"

"Where is she going?" asked Wei.

"I don't know! She might be going to the police. She might know where Dan is hiding. She might be going to tell him about the plan! We must catch her before she tells anyone! If she comes back to the office, catch her! Rob is following her to the metro station now."

Harry hung up. Then, he called Rob.

"Can you still see her?"

"Yes! She's on the platform. I'm going to get in the same train carriage as her. Then I'll catch her when she walks out of the station!"

# CHAPTER EIGHT

Nancy got off the train and ran towards the exit. She ran up the stairs. It was starting to get dark. She could see Victoria Peak in front of her.

*I hope he's in his new apartment, she* thought. *I'm sure he will be there. I'm nearly there.*

Rob hurried through the rush hour crowds. He could see a red coat a few metres in front of him. He had seen Nancy when he went to the office. He had said his name was Tim. He had said he worked at the Australian Embassy. Nancy had believed him.

Rob's phone rang. It was Harry.

Have you caught her? asked Harry.

"I'm following her," said Rob. "She's going to that new apartment block on the Peak."

"Catch her!" shouted Harry.

"I will! I'm waiting for her to go down an empty street so no one sees me."

"A car will be waiting for you in the street at the side of the apartment block. Catch her before she can go inside!"

Rob hung up and started running towards Nancy. The sky was dark, but there was a lot of light from the streetlights and from the windows of apartments in the tall apartment buildings. He ran fast.

Just before she reached the building, Nancy heard someone running behind her. She turned around just as the man grabbed her and pulled her into a side street. A car was waiting. It was a large black car. The man pushed her into the car, then he got in and the car drove off.

# CHAPTER NINE

The car was moving slowly through the early evening traffic. Nancy tried to open the door, but it was locked.

"You can't escape Nancy," said the man.

She turned to him and shouted, "Let me out!"

He smiled at her. This made Nancy angrier. She punched his arm.

He laughed at her again. Nancy's mobile phone started to ring.

Rob grabbed her bag and took out the phone. She tried to take it off him, but he pushed her away. He turned the phone off and put it in his pocket.

"Give me that!" she shouted.

"Why? So you can call the police? Don't be stupid," said Rob.

Nancy turned away and looked out of the window. It was raining.

*What can I do?* she thought. *I should have called the police when I heard the men talking in the apartment. It's too late now.*

The car stopped outside the apartment block. Rob pushed Nancy through the doors and into the elevator. The elevator stopped on the 39th floor. Rob opened the door of 39B and pushed Nancy inside.

Nancy looked around. It was a big apartment. It was empty. There were no sofas, chairs or tables. There were ceiling to floor windows with views across the city.

"So, this is Nancy," said a voice.

Nancy turned around and looked into a room on the right. There was a man sitting on the floor with a computer in front of him. He stood up.

"I'm Harry. It's a pleasure to meet you. Please, sit down," he said.

"Enjoy the view. We'll be leaving at eleven pm."

"Where are we going?" she shouted.

Harry laughed. "It's a secret. It's a surprise."

Rob was walking into the living room. There was no one behind Nancy. She turned around and ran to the front door. She pushed on the door. It was locked.

Rob ran towards her, grabbed her and pushed her into the living room. He pulled out a gun and pointed it at Nancy.

"If you try to escape again, I'll kill you," he said angrily. "Sit down and don't move!"

Nancy sat down on the floor. She closed her eyes.

*How can I get out of this?* she thought.

# CHAPTER TEN

Dan looked out of the window. He looked at his watch. 11:30pm.

*Time to go,* he thought. He put his coat on and fastened the buttons. He put his hat on. Then, he picked up two bags of money and his briefcase. He stood for a few seconds and looked out over the city.

*I'll miss this city,* he thought. *I'll miss my life here. Maybe I can come back someday.*

He thought about Nancy and his employees again. *I'll write to Nancy when I get back to Australia. She will probably hate me, but I hope she can forgive me someday.*

Then he turned away from the window, walked through the dark apartment to the front door, and walked out into the hallway. He looked around. The hallway was empty.

He got in the elevator and went down to the lobby. He walked out of the building and hurried towards the harbour.

On the yacht, Jason poured himself a large glass of whisky. He drank it all and then poured another glass. He walked up and down the small living room. He couldn't sit down. He was feeling nervous.

*They will be here soon,* he thought.

He heard a car drive into the harbour. He walked up onto the deck of the boat. He saw a large black car coming towards his boat.

The car stopped. Harry and four people got out of the car.

*They are here,* he thought.

Harry and the others climbed onto the boat. Jason shook hands with Harry. Then, he noticed a woman.

"Who is she?" he asked.

"A troublemaker," said Paul. "We're going to kill her too."

Jason was shocked. "Oh, right. OK. Would anyone like a drink before Dan gets here?"

*I'm making a big mistake,* he thought. *I shouldn't do this to Dan. But it's too late now.*

He took them into the living area of the boat and poured them all some whisky.

He looked at Nancy.

"Would you like a drink too?"

She nodded. She was in shock. *They are going to kill me too?* she thought.

About fifteen minutes later, Jason went onto the deck of the boat. He saw Dan running towards him. He waved to him.

"Dan, over here! Dan, my friend! How are you?" he said.

"Jason, thank you. Thank you for this," said Dan as he climbed onto the boat. The men shook hands.

"Have you got the money?" said Jason.

"Yes. It's in this bag," said Dan. He gave Jason one of the bags.

Jason took the bag. He put it in a box on the deck next to the lounge seat.

"I'll count it later. Come on, let's have a drink before we go."

Dan walked down the steps into the living area. Jason followed him.

"What? What's this?" shouted Dan. He turned around and looked at Jason. Jason closed the door behind him.

"Some people wanted to see you," said Jason.

"Hello Dan," said Harry. "So, you thought you could run away from me?"

"What?" Dan could not believe it. He looked around.

"Jason, what is going on?"

"Jason told me about your plan," said Harry. "He was in trouble with us too. He wanted to help himself."

Dan looked at Jason. "You told them? I don't believe this!"

"Sorry Dan," said Jason.

"But Jason is stupid," said Harry. "He trusted me. That was a big mistake. You see, we are going to kill him too."

Jason looked at Harry. "What? But, but...you said..."

Harry laughed. "Jason, you fool! Of course I'm going to kill you too. You know too much!"

Jason walked towards Harry. "Wait a minute, you said…"

Rob pulled out a gun and pointed it at Jason.

"Don't move," he said. Jason looked at the gun and stopped moving.

Dan looked around the room. In a corner, he saw Nancy.

"Nancy! What are you doing here?"

"She is a fool too. She tried to help you. She tried to find you. Of course, we are going to kill her too," said Harry. "When we are out of the harbour and in the sea, we will hit you all and throw you in the water. No one will find you."

He looked at Dan. "And everyone thinks you are already dead. They think you jumped off a bridge. So no one will look for you."

Harry looked at Paul.

"Time to go," he said. "Start the engine."

"Wait!" said Nancy

Everyone looked at her.

"What is it?" said Rob.

"I drank a lot of whisky. I feel sick. Can I go to the toilet? If I don't go to the toilet, I might be sick," she said. "Can I go before the boat starts moving?"

Everyone looked at each other. "If she's sick, the boat will smell," said Rob. "I don't want to sit in a smelly boat."

"OK, go to the toilet. Be quick," said Harry. "Rob, go with her. Stand outside the door so she can't escape."

Nancy and Rob walked to the toilet. Nancy went in and locked the door.

"Hurry up," said Rob.

*What am I going to do?* thought Nancy. *I have to stop the boat. I can't let them take the boat out of the harbour. They will kill us.*

Nancy looked around the room. It was very small. There was only a toilet and a sink. She switched the tap on. The sound of water running filled the air. There was a cabinet under the sink. She opened it. On the right side of the cabinet, there were towels. On the left side, there was a large black bag. She opened the bag and looked inside.

*Lights! Emergency flares!* she thought. She looked at the walls. There was a window at the top of the wall above the toilet.

*Can I open that window?* she thought.

"Hey! Hurry up!" shouted Rob outside.

"OK!" shouted Nancy. "Just give me a few more minutes."

Very quietly, she stood on the toilet and reached up to the window. The window opened easily.

"What are you doing in there?" shouted Rob.

"I'm on the toilet!" said Nancy.

Very quietly, she put a flare through the window. The bright light lit up the sky. Rob started banging on the door.

"Come on! Hurry up! If you don't hurry up, I'm coming in!"

Nancy didn't answer. She put another flare through the window.

Then, she climbed out of the window. People were looking at the boat. After about three minutes, she could see the harbour police car driving very quickly towards the boat. She waved both hands above her head.

From the window below, she heard Rob break through the door.

"Hey! She's gone!" he screamed.

"Help!" shouted Nancy to the police. "Help!"

Harry and the other men ran up the steps and out onto the deck. Harry saw the police car.

"What? I don't believe this!" shouted Harry. "Run everyone! Run!"

Two policemen jumped out of the police car and started running to the boat.

"Stop those men!" shouted Nancy, pointing to Harry and his men. "They are criminals!"

Harry and his men jumped into their car and drove off very quickly through the harbour area.

One of the policemen called for help, but it was too late. They had gone.

People from the other boats in the harbour started running towards the boat.

"What's happened?" they shouted. "What's going on?"

A policeman walked over to Nancy. "Come on. Let's take you to the police station. You can tell us everything that happened," he said.

"Yes, of course," said Nancy. She walked over to the police car. Soon, the car was driving through the city to the police station.

# CHAPTER ELEVEN

"Nancy, there's a letter for you," said May as she passed Nancy's desk.

"Thanks May," said Nancy. Nancy had been working at a new company for six months. It was summer now. She was trying to forget about the trouble with Dan. After the night on the yacht, she hadn't heard from him.

She looked at the envelope.

*It's from Australia,* she thought. She opened it and read it.

*---Dear Nancy,*

*I'm really sorry for everything that happened. I was in trouble. As you know, I had many apartments in Hong Kong. A man offered me an apartment for half price. I found out there was a gang. The leader of the gang was Harry. Of course, you remember him. He planned to kill you and Jason and me.*

*Harry and his gang were forcing older people out of their apartments and buying them for very low prices. I was so stupid. I thought I could be a hero. I thought I could help these people. So I didn't go to the police. I went to Harry and said 'I know everything.'*

*Harry said 'I will kill you.' I escaped, but I knew he was looking for me. I knew he would find me. I panicked. I didn't know what to do. Then, I had an idea. If they thought I jumped from the bridge and killed myself, I could escape. I was scared. I didn't plan anything carefully. I took some money out of the company bank account. I left my car on the bridge. Then I jumped into the water. I had a lifejacket on, so I was OK. But everyone thought I was dead. Then, I went to my new apartment to hide. The next morning, I called Jason and asked him to help me. He said 'I will help you if you pay me'. But he was in trouble with the group too. He lied to me. I put some money in the bag and gave it to Jason when I went to the yacht. Of course, I didn't give him all the money. I had most of it in my briefcase and the other bag.*

*That night, the police took Jason and me to the police station. I told them everything. The police said, 'You should leave Hong Kong. The group is very dangerous and knows many bad people. You should return to Australia.' So I left Hong Kong the next day.*

*I must say sorry to you Nancy. I caused you much trouble. You were in great danger because of me. And I must say thank you. Thanks to you, I am alive. You saved my life. You saved all our lives.*

*There was some money left in the company bank account. I'd like you to have it. It's about $200,000. It will be in your bank account by the end of the month.*

*I'm going to start another business here in Australia soon. I know that you must be very angry with me, but I'd like you to come and work for me here in Australia. If you would like to work with me, please let me know. Of course, I understand if you don't want to.*

*Once again, I'm very sorry. And thank you.*
*Dan---*


Nancy put the letter down. She closed her eyes.

*I don't know what to think,* she thought. *Who is Dan? I still don't know him well. We went out for dinner a few times. We had a nice time. I thought he was a nice man, and he was a very kind boss. But why didn't he go to the police when he had trouble? Why did he run away? Why didn't he tell me? I worked for him for a long time, but I still don't really know him.*

She read the letter once more. *Would I like to work in Australia? Would I like to work with Dan again?*

She put the letter down on the desk and closed her eyes.

*Yes, I think I would,* she thought. *But not yet.*

# THANK YOU

Thank you for reading Time to Go. (Word count: 8,238) We hope you enjoyed it.

There are quizzes about this book on our free study site I Talk You Talk Press EXTRA. http://italk-youtalk.com

If you would like to read more graded readers, please visit our website http://www.italkyoutalk.com

Other Level 3 graded readers include
A Dangerous Weekend
A Holiday to Remember
Akiko and Amy Part 1
Akiko and Amy Part 2
Akiko and Amy Part 3
Be My Valentine
Different Seas
Enjoy Your Business Trip
Enjoy Your Homestay
I Need a Friend
Old Jack's Ghost Stories from England (1)
Old Jack's Ghost Stories from England (2)
Old Jack's Ghost Stories from Ireland
Old Jack's Ghost Stories from Japan
Old Jack's Ghost Stories from Scotland

Old Jack's Ghost Stories from Wales
Party Time!
Stories for Christmas
The Curse
The Diary
Together Again
Who is Holly?

# ABOUT THE AUTHOR

I Talk You Talk Press is an award-winning Japan-based publisher of language textbooks, graded readers and language learning/teaching resources.

Our team is made up of highly experienced language teachers and translators, who have all studied at least one additional language to an advanced level.

This experience enables us to design our materials from the perspective of both the teacher and the learner. We consult with both teachers and language learners when designing our textbooks and graded readers, and test our materials extensively in the classroom before publication.

We are a fast-growing press, and currently publish graded readers for learners of English. We publish new graded readers monthly.

In 2019, we won first prize in the Upper Intermediate and Advanced Category of the Language Learner Literature Award and the Finalist prize in the Intermediate Category.

www.ingramcontent.com/pod-product-compliance
Lightning Source LLC
Chambersburg PA
CBHW022349040426
42449CB00006B/799